KU-628-598

Martyn Forrester

LAUGH YOUR HEAD OFF!

**Hysterical and historical
jokes and facts
A REVOLUTIONARY guide for kids**

Illustrated by Judy Brown

PUFFIN BOOKS

PUFFIN BOOKS

Published by the Penguin Group

27 Wrights Lane, London W8 5TZ, England

Viking Penguin Inc., 40 West 23rd Street, New York, New York 10010, USA

Penguin Books Australia Ltd, Ringwood, Victoria, Australia

Penguin Books Canada Ltd, 2801 John Street, Markham, Ontario, Canada L3R 1B4

Penguin Books (NZ) Ltd, 182-190 Wairau Road, Auckland 10, New Zealand

Penguin Books Ltd, Registered Offices: Harmondsworth, Middlesex, England

First published 1989

1 3 5 7 9 10 8 6 4 2

Filmset in Linotron Bodoni by

Rowland Phototypesetting (London) Limited

Printed and bound by

Cox and Wyman Ltd, Reading

Introduction

'Ello, 'ello,
You didn't know that you could speak
French, did you? But *introduction* is
the French word for 'introduction' (I
think) – so there you are. How good are
you at French history though, clever
clogs? I mean, do you know:

What's a guillotine?
A French chopping centre.

Why was King Louis XVI buried in
Paris?
Because he was dead.

Never mind if you didn't get the
answers right. That's what this book is
for – to teach thick planks like you. So
don't worry if you don't know what
happened in 1789. Me, I can't even
remember what happened last night.

Laugh Your Head Off! only teaches the bits of French history that you really need to know. Like, that the thinnest French emperor was Napoleon Boneypart, and that *lagoon* is the French word for idiot. As for France itself, the only thing I know about it is that I'm glad I wasn't born there – I can't speak a word of French.

This book is full of hysterical jokes and facts which will revolutionize your knowledge of French. Rave at the Revolution, jeer at the jokes and astound your classmates.

Your (totally honest! French) Editor

Revolutionary facts about the French . . .

● The French eat more cheese per head each year than any other nation.

● According to a survey carried out at Madame Tussauds, the most popular person in history was Joan of Arc.

● April Fool's Day is known as Fish Day in France.

● Steel expands when it is hot, making the Eiffel Tower 15 centimetres (6 inches) taller in summer than it is in winter.

● The kilt did not originate in Scotland, but in France.

● The most common surname in France is Martin.

- The word 'leotard' comes from Jacques Leotard, the French trapeze artiste who invented the one-piece garment.

- Châteaubriand steak is named after vicomte de Chateaubriand, the gourmet ambassador to Britain.

- A French actor named Pierre Messie could make his hair stand on end at will.

- The word 'biscuit' comes from the French *bis cuit*, which means 'twice cooked'. To preserve them for long periods, the original biscuits had to be cooked twice.

- A Frenchwoman, Madame de la Bresse, left a large sum of money in her will to provide clothes for snowmen.

- The French eat about five hundred million snails a year.

• It is considered very bad luck by the French to eat at a table of thirteen people. In Paris, a group of people once earned their living by attending dinner parties where the numbers needed bumping up to fourteen. They were known as *quatorzes*.

• The earliest form of lawn tennis was played by French monks.

Revolutionary facts about France . . .

● Nowhere in France is situated more than 500 kilometres (310 miles) from the sea.

● In Pas-de-Calais, France, there is a river named Aa.

● There is also a small village called Y in France.

• In some parts of Paris there are flush toilets for dogs.

• The Channel between England and France gets wider by one foot each year.

• The most expensive cheese in the world comes from France and is called *barratte*.

● The largest dinosaur egg ever
discovered was in France. It was as big
as a rugby ball.

● There are six million skeletons buried
in the catacombs beneath Paris. The
chambers were originally quarries used
by the Romans over 2,000 years ago.

15

Send your French teacher mad in one easy lesson!

You will not find any of these translations in your French/English dictionary. But try them out in your next French lesson and see how long it is before steam comes out of your poor teacher's ears . . .

FRENCH	ENGLISH
champagne	fake window
mal de mer	nail the horse
coup de grâce	cut the grass
entre chat	entry for the cat
entrez	on the tray
amoureuse	her hammer
poussinière	the cat's in there
ouvrez la fenêtre	hoover the furniture

une plume de mon oncle	a monocled plum
la mer	she horse
fil à plomb	feel a plum
pas de tout	father of twins
non merci	no mercy
s'il vous plaît	silver plate
défense d'afficher	defend the fishes
dans le main	the main dance
deux enfants	baby ducks
faux pas	an enemy of the father
poisson blanquette	poison blanket
Je ne comprends pas	I do not understand father
hors de combat	horse of war
moi aussi	I am an Australian

Learn 23 French words in 23 seconds!

You'll really impress your friends and family when you ask them to read the words below in English, and tell them you will give the French translations, without making a single mistake. Until, that is, about the fifth word . . .

ENGLISH	FRENCH
biscuit	*le biscuit*
blouse	*la blouse*
bracelet	*le bracelet*
centre	*le centre*
certain	*certain*
chance	*la chance*
direction	*la direction*
distance	*la distance*
garage	*le garage*
guide	*le guide*
message	*le message*

million	*le million*
nature	*la nature*
police	*la police*
possible	*possible*
sauce	*la sauce*
simple	*simple*
table	*la table*
train	*le train*
vase	*le vase*
village	*le village*
voyage	*le voyage*
zero	*le zero*

Revolutionary facts about French history . . .

● During the Franco–Prussian War of 1870–71, when Paris was under siege, balloons were used to carry post from the beleaguered city. Over three million letters were delivered by the very first airmail service.

● André Jacques Garnerin made the first parachute descent on 22 October 1797, from a balloon over Parc Monceau in Paris. The first thing he did after landing was to vomit violently.

● The turkey was first imported to France by Jesuit priests, and is still known in some French dialects as a *jesuite*.

• In 1808 two Frenchmen fought a
pistol duel in hot-air balloons
suspended over Paris. One man
plummeted more than a thousand feet
to his death.

• In one short period in the Middle
Ages, over 30,000 cases of werewolfery
were reported in France.

● In 1804 at Toulouse there was a shower of frogs during a storm. Roads and fields were blocked with the creatures.

● French women only got the vote in 1944.

● Arnold Bennett, author of *The Old Wives' Tale*, died of typhoid in Paris in 1931 after drinking a glass of water to prove that the local water was perfectly safe to drink.

● It was fashionable in the fourteenth century for French ladies to wear corsets over their normal clothes.

● In the eight years between 1601 and 1609, some 2,000 French noblemen were killed in duels. Cyrano de Bergerac (no relation to Jim Bergerac), the French poet and swordsman, fought and won 1,000 duels over insults about his huge nose. During one particular three-month period, his sword passed through an average of four people each week.

● The first cross-Channel air flight was made by Blanchard and Jeffries on 7 January 1785. The trip took two hours and at the end the intrepid balloonists had to throw most of their clothes overboard to prevent their craft from losing height.

● In 1740, a cow in France was found guilty of witchcraft and hanged.

● The first artificial hand was invented by a Frenchman in 1551.

● During the Napoleonic Wars, a monkey was hanged after being found guilty of being a French spy.

• Courtiers at the Palace of Versailles considered it rude to knock on doors — so they grew the little fingernail of their left hand so that they could scratch on them instead.

• In 1635 the sale of tobacco was banned in France. Unfortunately, it could still be obtained with a doctor's prescription.

• Nicotine is named after the French ambassador to Portugal, who brought the evil substance tobacco to France in the 1500s.

Revolutionary facts about Louis XIV . . .

● Louis XIV (born 5 September 1638) was one of the vainest men in history, but he was also bald. He vowed that no one but his personal barber would ever see his bald head. The Royal hairdresser had to sneak the king's curly wig into his bedroom early each morning, and collect it late at night.

● The most expensive robe ever worn belonged to Louis XIV. It was encrusted with diamonds and cost one-sixth of the value of the Palace of Versailles.

● Madame Tallien, a member of Louis XIV's court, was in the habit of bathing in crushed strawberries whenever they were in season.

- King Louis XIV originated and was the first to wear high-heeled shoes.

- King Richard III and Louis XIV were born with teeth.

● Louis XIV had 413 beds. The beautifully carved and gilded masterpieces were dotted about France, so that wherever he travelled he could always sleep in his own bed. His bed in the Palace of Versailles had velvet curtains with the 'Triumph of Venus' woven in gold.

● Louis XIV ordered that no members of his court should sit in chairs which had arms.

● Queen Marie Antoinette and King Louis XIV of France might have escaped execution had it not been for a twist of fate in 1791. While attempting to escape from France, the horses of their coach had to be changed. Deciding that they would get out of the coach to wait while the horses were changed, the king and queen were recognized and began their journey to the next world. Had they remained inside the coach, they would have escaped. If it had been raining, for instance, maybe Marie Antoinette would not have lost her pretty head.

● Louis XIV had only three baths in his whole life.

● Louis XIV once had a frightening experience. While he was putting a sock on, his toe fell off.

● William Buckland, nineteenth-century Dean of Westminster, ate Louis XIV's embalmed heart for dinner one evening.

Revolutionary facts about French kings and queens . . .

● The most expensive dress in history was made for Marie de Medici (1573–1643), Queen of France. It was embroidered with 3,000 diamonds and 39,000 pearls, and would be worth £10,000,000 million today. The Queen wore the dress only once, at the baptism of her son in 1606.

● King Louis Philippe fled to Switzerland during the French Revolution and taught mathematics at a college in Reichnau under an assumed name. He became ruler of France again in 1830, but abdicated in 1848. He and his wife fled the country disguised as 'Mr and Mrs Smith'.

• King Louis IX of France died of the plague in 1244 at the age of twenty-nine. Then, during his funeral service, he sat up in his coffin . . . He went on to reign for another twenty-six years, and was eventually declared a saint.

• Louis XIII was once bled forty-seven times in one month by his physician.

• When Marie Antoinette's horoscope
was cast shortly after her birth, it
predicted such disaster that a party to
celebrate her birth was cancelled.

• The Marquis de Pelier was
imprisoned for fifty years for daring to
whistle at Marie Antoinette.

• William III (1650–1702) of England, grandson of Charles I, was also William IV of Normandy, William III of Holland, William II of Scotland and William I of Ireland.

• Charles VIII of France had six toes on one foot. He introduced a fashion for shoes with square tips so that nobody would notice his deformity.

• Marie Antoinette lost her hair shortly after marrying Louis XIV and took to wearing elaborate wigs. When she was imprisoned during the French Revolution, her wig was taken away from her and she became a laughing-stock. She was allowed to wear a white cap to the guillotine, but when it was removed at the last minute the crowd hooted with laughter.

• William the Conqueror was buried at Rouen in 1087. In 1562, vandals broke into his tomb and stole everything, except his thigh bone. During the French Revolution, that, too, was stolen.

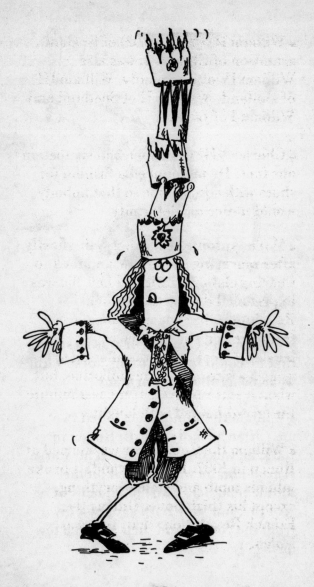

● William the Conqueror was so strong that he could leap on to his horse while wearing a full suit of armour.

● William the Conqueror killed two men after he had died. In Rouen in 1087, he was out riding when his horse reared and he was impaled on the saddle pommel. Two embalmers were sent for, but they both caught a fever from the corpse and died within a few days.

● To keep Louis XV's love, his mistress, Madame de Pompadour, lived on a diet of vanilla, truffles and celery, all of which were meant to have special properties.

● Catherine de Médicis commanded that all women at the French court should have waists that measured no more than 34 centimetres (13 inches).

● King Henry III of France used to hang a basket loaded with small dogs around his neck.

● Accents were first introduced into French writing during the reign of Louis XIII.

● King Henry IV used the Grande Galerie at the Louvre Museum for indoor fox hunts on wet days. To make the scenery more realistic, trees, grass and rocks were brought in and scattered around the room.

● Charles VIII of France was too polite for his own good. In 1498, while escorting his wife into a tennis court, he looked at her rather than at where he was going and fractured his skull on a low beam. He died soon afterwards.

● The Mona Lisa was originally bought by King Francis I of France in 1517 to hang in his bathroom. The estimated value of the painting today is £35 million.

● The Palace of Versailles has over one thousand fountains in its grounds.

● Charles the Simple was the grandson of Charles the Bald. Both were rulers of France.

LAUGH YOUR HEAD OFF...

Where were the kings and queens of France crowned?
On their heads.

What was the first thing Louis XIV did on coming to the throne?
He sat down.

How long was Louis XIV on the throne?
The same length as he was off it.

TEACHER: At your age I could name all the French monarchs in the correct order.
PUPIL: *Yes, but in those days there'd only been three or four of them.*

Who is known as the chiropodist king?
William the Corncurer.

Which king was full of chestnuts?
William the Conkerer.

TEACHER: Were there any great men
born at the Palace of Versailles?
PUPIL: *No, only little babies.*

Revolutionary facts about Napoleon Bonaparte . . .

● Napoleon Iced Cake is named after the Emperor, who had a sweet tooth.

● Napoleon Bonaparte designed the national flag of Italy.

● Baron Dominique Larry, Napoleon's surgeon, could amputate a man's leg in fourteen seconds.

- Napoleon Bonaparte suffered from ailurophobia, a fear of cats.

- The last American descendant of Napoleon Bonaparte died in New York after tripping over a dog lead in Central Park.

- Napoleon used to travel in a bulletproof coach.

- Napoleon's wife, Marie Louise, could move her ears at will and even turn them inside out.

● After the Battle of Waterloo, people were frightened of growing or wearing violets because they had been Napoleon's favourite flower.

● Gin was used medically at the Battle of Waterloo. Count Blucher, Field Marshal of the Prussian forces, was thrown from his horse and revived with a rub of the alcohol. He went on to help Wellington defeat Napoleon.

• Autographs are big business. Emperor Napoleon left 250,000 signatures on various documents, each one worth about £40,000.

• Napoleon died in exile on the island of St Helena on 5 May 1821, possibly of wallpaper poisoning. His room was decorated with green paper, the pigment of which was the poisonous copper arsenite. Whatever the cause of his death, the British did not release his body to the French until twenty days later.

LAUGH
YOUR
HEAD
OFF...

FIRST BOY: Napoleon conquered France, conquered Russia and conquered Italy.
SECOND BOY: *Why did he stop?*
FIRST BOY: He ran out of conkers.

JACQUES: Who was the thinnest emperor?
ANNIQUE: *Napoleon Boneypart.*

Who lost at Waterloo and exploded?
Napoleon Blownapart.

FIRST GIRL: Your history teacher seems to know the French Revolution inside out.
SECOND GIRL: *She should do. She's so old, she was probably there.*

Where did Napoleon keep his armies?
Up his sleevies.

BOY: My great-grandfather fought with Napoleon, my grandfather fought with the French and my father fought with the Germans.

GIRL: *It seems as if your family couldn't get along with anybody.*

BOY: Our teacher was telling us about the Battle of Waterloo today.

MOTHER: *What did he say?*

BOY: He claimed he was lucky to have escaped with such a minor wound.

TEACHER: What is the difference between the death rate during the French Revolution and the death rate today?

PUPIL: *It's the same, sir – one death per person.*

Revolutionary facts about six English kings who were born in France . . .

• Henry II was born in Le Mans in 1133.

• Richard II was born in Bordeaux in 1367.

• Edward IV was born in Rouen in 1442.

• William the Conqueror was born in Falaise in 1027.

• William Rufus was born in Normandy in 1058.

• Stephen was born in Blois in 1096.

LAUGH YOUR HEAD OFF...

Why did Henry VIII have so many wives?
Because he liked to chop and change.

TEACHER: In what battle was King Harold killed in 1066?
PUPIL: *His last one.*

TEACHER: Why was King Louis XVI buried in Paris?
PUPIL: *Because he was dead.*

What were Anne Boleyn's last words?
'I think I'll go for a walk around the block.'

What's fruity and burns cakes?
Alfred the Grape.

Some English monarchs were Henry
VII, Henry VIII, Edward VI and Mary.
Who came after Mary?
The little lamb.

What did Sir Walter Ralegh say when
he dropped his cloak before Queen
Elizabeth I?
'Step on it, kid.'

Lady Jane Grey
Had nothing to say;
What could she have said
After losing her head?

What did King John wear?
*Nothing. He lost everything in the
Wash.*

TEACHER: The ruler of Russia was called the Tsar and his wife was called the Tsarina. What were his children called?

PUPIL: *Tsardines?*

Down memory lane

The hard thing about history is remembering the dates. But here is a revolutionary way of helping them to stick in your mind. Make up silly poems like these that rhyme with the date and you'll be top of the history class before you can say 'knife' – or even 'guillotine'.

French Revolution: 1789
In seventeen hundred and eighty-nine
The king got the chop but the workers were fine.

Relief of Mafeking: 1901
The siege of Mafeking was undone
In the year of nineteen hundred and one.

Boston Tea Party: 1773
In seventeen hundred and
seventy-three
Bostonians filled their harbour
with tea.

Spanish Armada: 1588
The Spanish Armada? Its special date
Is fifteen hundred and eighty-eight.

Columbus discovered America: 1492
In fourteen hundred and ninety-two
Columbus sailed the ocean blue.

Death of William IV: 1837
William the Fourth went up to
Heaven
In eighteen hundred and
thirty-seven.

LAUGH YOUR HEAD OFF...

What stands in the middle of Paris and smells nice?
The Eiffel Flower.

What monster became President of France?
Charles de Ghoul.

Who lived in a house with two bathrooms and painted cancan girls?
Two Loos Lautrec.

What's wrapped in Clingfilm and terrorizes Paris?
The lunch-pack of Notre Dame.

How do you say 'idiot' in French?
Lagoon.

What stands in the middle of Paris and wobbles?
The Trifle Tower.

TEACHER: Why does the Eiffel Tower stand in Paris?
PUPIL: *Because it can't sit down.*

TEACHER: Can you tell me what happened in 1789?
PUPIL: *I can't even remember what happened last night.*

TEACHER: Where in France does it never rain?
PUPIL: *Under an umbrella.*

TEACHER: How would you describe the rain in the French Alps?
PUPIL: *Little drops of water falling from the sky.*

TEACHER: What is your favourite country?
PUPIL: *Czechoslovakia.*
TEACHER: Spell it.
PUPIL: *On second thoughts, I think I prefer France.*

What do you get if you cross the Channel with a sailing ship?
To the other side.

What do you call an English general at Waterloo carrying a telescope?
Seymour.

What do you get if you cross a flat fish with Napoleon Bonaparte?
The flounder of modern France.

What's purple and close to France?
Grape Britain.

FRED: I'm glad I wasn't born in France.
BERT: *Why's that?*
FRED: I can't speak a word of French.

TEACHER: In what year did Robespierre die?
PUPIL: *Die? I didn't even know he was sick.*

HERE COMES NAPOLEON - RUN FOR YOUR LIVES by GENERAL PANIC

ESCAPE FROM THE GUILLOTINE

THE CHARGE OF THE LIGHT BRIGADE

LIFE IN NAPOLEON'S ARMY by REGGIE MENT AND KIT BAGG

CAUGHT UP IN THE REVOLUTION by M.I. GLADYS ALLOVER

ESCAPE ACROSS THE CHANNEL by WENDY GO

NAPOLEON'S GREATEST BATTLES by Ida Clare War

FIGHTING FOR LIBERTY by WARREN PEACE

THE FRENCH MUSKETEER'S BULLET

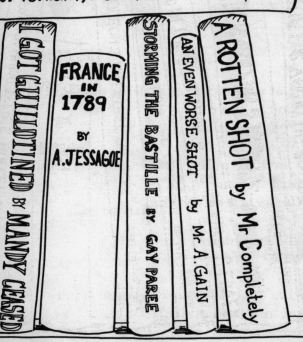

JUSTIN de NICOTIME

...ACKER WAYTHROUGH

...OT TONIGHT, JOSEPHINE BY Miles Apart

I GOT GUILLOTINED BY MANDY CEASED

FRANCE IN 1789 BY A.JESSAGOE

STORMING THE BASTILLE BY GAY PAREE

(AN EVEN WORSE SHOT) by Mr A. GAIN

A ROTTEN SHOT by Mr Completely

69

What would you get if all the cars in
France were red?
A red carnation.

What's the quickest way to the Gare du
Nord station?
Run as fast as you can.

Who was Joan of Arc?
Noah's wife.

What's the difference between Noah's
Ark and Joan of Arc?
*One was made of wood, and the other
was Maid of Orleans.*

Knock, knock.
Who's there?
Noah.
Noah who?
Noah good book about the French
Revolution when I see one.

What's three feet tall and rides on the
Paris underground?
A Metro-gnome.

What weighed twenty stone and
haunted Paris?
The Fat-Tum of the Opera.

What's a guillotine?
A French chopping centre.

And a bit more history . . .

Why did the Romans build straight roads?
So the Britons couldn't hide around the corners.

Who ruled Gaul and kept catching colds?
Julius Sneezer.

What's Roman and climbs walls?
IV.

What happened to Boadicea when she lost the battle?
Julius seized 'er.

What did Caesar say when Brutus stabbed him?
'Ouch.'

OUCH!

Which mouse was a Roman Emperor?
Julius Cheeser.

TEACHER: When was Rome built?
PUPIL: *At night.*
TEACHER: Why do you say that?
PUPIL: *Because I read that Rome wasn't built in a day.*

What did they call Julius Caesar on a foggy night in Scotland?
A Roman in the gloaming.

TEACHER: What did Julius Caesar do before crossing the Rubicon?
PUPIL: *Get in the boat.*

What was the most remarkable achievement of the Romans?
Learning Latin.

How was the Roman Empire cut in half?
With a pair of Caesars.

Revolutionary
rhymes . . .

There was a young schoolgirl of Rhyl,
Whose general knowledge was nil;
She thought Joan of Arc
Navigated the craft
That landed on Ararat's hill.

A French poodle espied in the hall
A pool an umbrella'd let fall;
He said: 'Ah, oui, oui,
This time it's not me,
But I'm bound to be blamed for it all.'

LAUGH YOUR HEAD OFF...

Knock, knock.
Who's there?
Anatole.
Anatole who?
Anatole me you're a pain in the neck.

Knock, knock.
Who's there?
Sacha.
Sacha who?
Sacha lot of jokes about the French
Revolution.

Knock, knock.
Who's there?
Celeste.
Celeste who?
Celeste time I lend you money.

Knock, knock.
Who's there?
Madame.
Madame who?
Madame finger's caught in the
guillotine.

Knock, knock.
Who's there?
Yolande.
Yolande who?
Yolande me a few francs, I'll pay you
back later.

Knock, knock.
Who's there?
Isabelle.
Isabelle who?
Isabelle necessary on a bicycle?

Knock, knock.
Who's there?
Eugenie.
Eugenie who?
Eugenie from the bottle will grant you a wish.

Knock, knock.
Who's there?
Annie.
Annie who?
Anniversary of the French Revolution.

Knock, knock.
Who's there?
Nadya.
Nadya who?
Nadya head if you understand me.

Knock, knock.
Who's there?
Michelle.
Michelle who?
Michelle had a crab inside it.

REVOLUTIONARY

RICHARD THE
LIONHEART WAS
THE WORLD'S
FIRST TRANSPLANT
PATIENT

TIP FOR FRENCH
ORAL EXAMS —
WHEN IN DOUBT,
MUMBLE

THE FRENCH NATIONAL ANTHEM
IS THE MAYONNAISE

FRENCH GRAFFITI

THE DARK AGES
WERE FULL OF
KNIGHTS

MONSOON IS A
FRENCH WORD
MEANING MISTER

X | O
O | O
O | X

WAS OLD KING COLE
THE FATHER OF
THE BLACK PRINCE?

MY TEACHER IS A
REDHEAD - NO HAIR
JUST A RED HEAD!

Revolutionary facts about the French Revolution . . .

● The composer of the French revolutionary anthem, *La Marseillaise*, had once been a strong supporter of the king.

• In 1789 the average life expectancy for males was 34 years 5 months, and for females 36 years 5 months.

• The metric system was devised during the French Revolution. It was based on the metre, which was calculated to be one ten-millionth part of the shortest distance along the earth's surface between the Pole and the Equator.

● French revolutionaries tried to establish a ten-day week.

● One French executioner got the sack after pawning his guillotine.

• During the French Revolution, the skins of guillotined aristocrats were tanned to make leather. One such hide was used as the binding for the new French Constitution.

• During the French Revolution, Madame Tussaud, later famous for her waxworks in London, used her model-making skills to make death masks for the victims of the guillotine.

You'll die laughing . . .

● The guillotine was first used on 25 April 1792, for the execution of a highwayman.

● The guillotine was said by its inventor, Dr Guillotine, to be a painless form of execution and that the victim felt nothing more than a chill on the back of the neck. We cannot tell how he knew this for no victim could ever explain how it felt.

● The last public execution by the guillotine occurred as late as June 1939 when murderer Eugen Weidmann lost his head in Paris at 4.50 a.m. on the seventeenth of that month.

● The last European witch was burned in Switzerland in 1782.

● French politician, Jacques Necker, had his dead wife's body placed in a large stone coffin filled with alcohol to preserve her. He visited the corpse every day.

● Joan of Arc was burned at the stake when she was nineteen.

● Eighteenth-century French actor Jean Marie Collot d'Herbois was such a bad actor that during a performance at Lyons he was actually booed off stage. Taking up another profession, he later returned as a Justice of the Peace during the French Revolution and ordered the death of 6,000 Lyons citizens. Revenge is sweet.

Revolutionary French general knowledge test

1. What colour is the red, white and blue French flag?

2. How far is it (in kilometres) from Paris to the capital city of France?

3. Who invented the wheel?

4. At what age was Louis XIV born?

5. How do you spell GUILLOTINE?

6. Marie Antoinette's favourite horse
was called Terry Wogan. True or false?

7. Who painted the Mona Lisa?
   Frank Bruno/Sugar Ray Leonard/
   Leonardo da Vinci

8. What day was the day before the day
after yesterday?

9. What does the smell of garlic look like?

10. What language do the French speak?